Bulletproof:
15 Laws for Unshakeable Confidence, Defeating Your Fears, and Conquering Your Goals
(Confidence Hacks and Mindsets)

By Patrick King
Dating and Social Skills Coach at
www.PatrickKingConsulting.com

D1111841

Table of Contents

Bulletproof: 15 Laws for Unshakeable Confidence, Defeating Your Fears, and Conquering Your Goals (Confidence Hacks and Mindsets)

Introduction

Confidence hasn't always come easily for me.

It probably started from my roots as a **fat kid**.

And when I say fat kid, I don't mean that I just had chubby cheeks. I mean that when I look back at an elementary school class photos, I was literally twice as wide the kids next to me.

I was large, rotund, and had rolls anywhere a little boy can have them... and some places they can't. **Michelin Man, anyone**?

So how do you expect that other children, insensitive out of naiveté, might have treated me? I was the (wide) butt of many a joke, and coming home holding back tears was a weekly occurrence.

However, let me be the primary example of how confidence isn't innate and is actually extremely learnable.

At some point in high school, puberty helped me shed most of the excess weight I had carried throughout my life, and I was gifted a new outlook that I previously never had... because people simply treated me better when I wasn't overweight. Both male and female. Anyone that's had a physical transformation can attest to the fact of treatment being far different when perceived levels of attraction change.

That was my first lesson in the realm of confidence – **the world we live in is shallow**. It just is, and as soon as you can wrap your head around that reality, you can start taking advantage of it in two distinct ways.

First, since the world is shallow, it was relatively easy to notice the change in feedback and signals I was getting from other people, which created upward spiral of confidence. I was able to internalize how people treated me because of my new exterior. In other words, because people treated me better and like someone with confidence, my confidence was able to grow.

Second, it's like when you wear a mask during Halloween – you feel incredibly empowered because you're playing someone else's role, and that someone else has the utmost of confidence. That role overshadows your insecurities so you are able to channel whoever and whatever you want. A thinner me was like a mask of the confident guy I had seen in movies my whole life, and it was very empowering.

But that's my story, and certainly not how everyone can internalize and grow their own confidence. In fact, few people probably have that specific sort of physical transformation scenario. But that only tells part of the story. Confidence is not as easy as just losing weight and getting a haircut.

If it was as simple as that, it would mean that confidence was directly correlated with physical attractiveness, and we all know people that prove that the opposite is true – sometimes, the most attractive people we know are also the most insecure.

So it is obvious that external changes can only take you so far and are only a piece of the overarching puzzle of confidence. But how do you gain confidence when you don't have anything to feel confident about? It's a serious **chicken and egg problem** with many people.

And yet that's the problem and question that I hope to answer in this book with my **15 laws for unshakeable confidence**. Confidence can't just appear out of thin air, and it must also skirt a thin line lest it veer into arrogance and overcompensation territory.

It must be rooted in reality, and also give recognition to flaws and vulnerabilities.

As the saying "all roads lead to Rome" goes, all things with unshakeable confidence begin and start with **internal mindsets grounded in objective reality that you define yourself.** Every word of that phrase is carefully selected and is important for reasons that you'll read later, and confidence is a process in itself.

When you can start to internalize and embody the 15 laws in this book, my hope is that you'll see exactly the path you need to take to achieve real confidence that doesn't nosedive after any negative comment, but that is also down to earth and realistic. This path in particular can be painful and frightening because it may force you face certain harsh truths about yourself, but the more you overcome the stronger you become. You'll survive the process and see that you can accomplish more than you previously thought possible – and that survival and process will also bolster your confidence.

When you reach a certain threshold of confidence and you are able to hold your head a few degrees higher than you ever were previously, you'll begin to truly recognize the importance and role of confidence in success. You'll be treated better, and people will just assume positive things about you. You'll just get further in life. It's not fair, but you might as well be primed to take advantage of people's perceptions.

You will see your own version of my fat kid story and how people will treat you differently with and without confidence. The difference can be startling, and only then will you begin to realize how strong confidence can literally change your life.

Law 1. Confidence is the gateway emotion.

It originally felt like a stretch to assert the following, but the more I think about it, the truer it becomes. **If you want to succeed in life, you simply need confidence.**

You can be as friendly as possible or the most interesting person in the world, but if you lack confidence and self-esteem, it simply doesn't matter because *people won't see it*.

Consider confidence a **gateway emotion.** Confidence allows everything that is good about you to shine through.

A charming person without confidence won't be charming, they will be in the corner waiting for someone to validate and speak to them. An attractive person of the opposite sex won't get dates because they would never take the initiative to talk to someone. A highly competent engineer would never rise in the ranks because they might not consider themselves a leader or worthy of a promotion.

In the end, it doesn't matter what degree or education you have, or how tall and great your hair is. **Without confidence, it's nothing. And with confidence, they are irrelevant.** We all have people in our lives that are impressive regardless of their lack of pedigree, and we all know people that have impressive pedigrees but underwhelm in real life.

Interesting how that works, isn't it? The rate at which you get promoted, get dates, or succeed in life is amazingly influenced by your confidence quotient.

Thankfully, confidence is the definition of learned behavior. Confidence right out of the womb isn't real confidence – we call that **delusional and arrogant**. It's based on nothing and has no foundation, and therefore can be smashed in a matter of seconds.

But **confidence as a process**, as I describe in this book, is incredibly strong and unshakeable. The process of growing true confidence comes from a recognition of what your real strengths and flaws are, and recognizing that neither of those, especially your flaws, define you as a person. A large part of the process is introspective and cataloging your strengths to recognize that you have **much** to be confident about.

All of social interaction is about the signals that you send to others. These combine to form an image of you and where you are in the invisible social hierarchy. It's not conscious, but we've all had the feeling of meeting someone that we just have zero interest in.

When you send out unconfident signals, where do you think you end up in the social hierarchy? How likely do you think you are to get what you want? How likely do you think you are to be taken advantage of or bullied? How likely do you think you will get ahead in life? If you're the bottom rung of the social hierarchy as a result of unconfident signals, people will simply feel less respect towards you.

If you project a high level of confidence, you will be perceived as being higher up than most people. People will treat you with more respect. People will give you the benefit of the doubt. Project the opposite and people may feel that they can get away with stepping all over you.

People will treat you differently if you have a higher level of confidence. In fact, you don't have to be the most educated, wealthy, or smartest person in the room. You only need to send the right confidence signals and people will 'read' into you all sorts of indicators of authority, credibility, power, and sexual attraction.

Of course, there's an inherent question of why people even respond so favorably to confidence. Is it just because it shows you have strength and forces respect? Not quite.

When people see a confident presence, it inspires them.

Everyone's lives are a reflection of the choices they have made, and a confident presence reminds people of the possibilities of their lives. It reminds them of what they can achieve if they make the right choices, and sometimes just the choice to be confident. It gives them hope. It gives them a role model to aspire to.

Imagine the opposite – how does an unconfident person make people feel? It makes them feel pity, negativity, or stuck in their own lives. Misery breeds company, and so does a lack of confidence. We don't want to be surrounded by people that life seems impossible for – we want to spend time with those that point us to the freedom and strength that we can choose.

If confidence can make people respect you and simultaneously make them feel good about themselves, it should be no surprise that confidence draws people like moths to a flame.

Successful people are confident.

Whether they started with nothing or were born with a silver spoon in their mouths, they still had goals that required confidence. It required a certain degree of believing in their potential and skills, even if they weren't so sure at the beginning.

To move up in your career, you need confidence in what your abilities are. To upgrade your love life, you need confidence in yourself that you are attractive and that someone will want to be with you.

If you are not confident, the world can be a hostile place. You can feel that life simply happens to you instead of you making things happen. It can be a downward spiral that can lead to discouragement, mediocre results, and ultimately a wasted life.

Are you looking for a life full of victories and possibilities? Or are you looking for a life that is basically stuck, mediocre, and essentially forgettable? You can either continue to make excuses or you can choose to start making progress by learning how to be confident. **Cross the threshold and enter the gateway.**

Law 2. Confidence creates magnetism.

People are attracted to others with confidence.

Is that a surprise? Confidence is all about taking control over your reality. It inspires and motivates people, and possessing the inner strength to impose your will to **make "it should" into "it will."**

Most of all, it reminds them others that they too can accomplish what confident people can.

Confidence serves a great role in inspiring because most people are actually **cowards**. I don't mean this in a derogatory manner.

Most people are simply driven more by their fear than their dreams and aspirations. They don't take action. They find excuses. They don't want to fail, and spend most of their time finding ways to avoid failing instead of thinking ahead and formulating how they can excel and soar.

Not surprisingly, most people lead lives of quiet desperation. They are content with living on the edges of their dreams and doing the same thing again and again. They basically settle for life as pigeons eating crumbs when they can be soaring high like eagles.

Confident people remind them that they have the inner strength to make things happen.

I don't care whether you are in a corporate boardroom, a bar, or a team huddle. The most confident person there is always the center of attention. The most confident person there is always at the spotlight. If you want to attract the right kind of attention so that you can be promoted more, get the right raises, or attract the attention of the opposite sex, it literally pays to be more confident.

Male confidence is crucial for sexual attraction.

As much as we would like to believe that we are rational and logical human beings who have evolved beyond our primal needs, deep down we are still apes. And with any grouping of apes, it is always the confident male who beats his chest the loudest who gets his pick of the women. That was the reality in the past, still is, and will continue to be the reality long into the future.

The main driver of this form of sexual selection was very biological. Females are attracted to males who can defend their young. Females are attracted to males who have the willpower and physical strength to get the resources necessary to sustain a family and support the next generation. It is all about self-interest. It is all about resource accumulation.

But fast forward a few million years to now, and there is still a certain part of the human psyche that hasn't really evolved all that much. As much as we would like to say that we have fancy degrees, great education and all this amazing technology, there is still that primordial part of the human brain that is attracted to the alpha male's ability to take care of material needs and provide defense. **Confidence is exactly how this is outwardly manifested.**

Business is all about confidence.

There are two ways to look at business. You can set up your business and try to avoid losing money, and simply stay in the black. Or you can set up your business with an eye towards soaring revenues that you alone collect. The latter requires a certain amount of risk and spirit, and confidence and belief in oneself are central ingredients.

If you want to take your business to the next level, you need to work with somebody who is confident enough and has the internal strength and willpower to do what is needed to make things happen for your business. They must believe in themselves that it can happen, or else it certainly won't.

Confidence will always be a raw ingredient to business success. People will always rather do business with somebody with a high level of confidence rather than somebody who is unsure of themselves.

If you have a million dollars to invest, who would you rather do business with? Somebody who tells you that things are possible and projects that air and spirit of confidence? Or somebody who is basically walking around with his tail between his legs and is afraid of loss? Someone who is confidence about their product, or is always worried about how their product falls short in the market? The difference is like night and day.

These confident people might not have the technical skills. They might not have the track record or experience, but it doesn't really matter. People read in to their confidence, their innate ability to find those raw materials needed later on to make things happen.

When you are more confident, people want to be around you. People like to be around winners and not losers. Losers are often equated with a low level of self-confidence, with self-doubt and timidness. They drag down the collective ability and capacity of everyone around them.

Confident people push the envelope. Confident people take the risk. Confident people make that leap of faith. Things happen when you are around confident people. Not only do you end up encouraging other people, but seeing their respect and admiration encourages you.

The secret to confidence and its attraction really boils down to an upward spiral. The more confident you are, the more you inspire other people. The more inspired other people are around you, the more confident you get.

All it takes is the decision to be more confident starting today.

Law 3. Diagnose your confidence drainers.

It's a charming notion that we are all the masters of our own **destiny**. That we determine our entire lives alone, without the influence of anyone or anything else. That we function primarily in the pursuit of our dreams and aspirations.

Well, this is truer for some people than others, but it's still a fairy tale that ignores the reality of past influences and external circumstances.

Baggage.

We are, as human beings, **products of our circumstances and products of our times.** The things that happened to you when you were a child or baby can impact the whole aspect of your life as you get older. This influence continues to produce effects all through your life.

It is easy to look at self-development and personal willpower as completely eradicating and replacing all previous influences. But if you believe this, you are settling on a pipe dream.

You have to make peace with the fact that your whole being, including your level of confidence, is a mix of both internal and external causes. By simply dismissing external causes, you are not doing yourself any favors. Their effects still linger and are real.

To achieve the level of confidence that you are looking for, you need to understand the **complicated interplay** between internal and external causes of confidence or the lack thereof. This enables you to work around the effects of external causes so you can get precisely what you are looking for as far as confidence is concerned.

And that's the first and foremost confidence drainer – the past, circumstances outside of our control, and how we grew up.

Another confidence drainer is **lack of awareness**.

If you are unaware that something is important, chances are that you will neglect it.

Everybody has to have some level of confidence. Simply dismissing it as unimportant in your life is one of the main causes of why people have such low levels of confidence. Ultimately, this harms them at many different levels. Remember that confidence is the gateway emotion, and the key to being able to show off the rest of your positive traits. Without confidence, your talents will live locked inside a shoebox, likely never to be discovered and opened.

Fear is another internal cause of lack of confidence. People would like to be more confident but they are just afraid of the consequences of going out on a limb. Even if you have the innate ability to do great things yet are so afraid of failure, you won't be able to take the right risks necessary to achieve greatness. You end up wasting your time (and your life) languishing on the edges of greatness but never really taking the plunge.

An **external** confidence drainer is **past negative experiences**. You may have had negative experiences ·in the past where you feel ashamed, embarrassed, or guilty. Regardless of the specific situation, you have to understand that continuing to feel bad about things that happened in the past is terrible for your confidence, and an unhealthy habit in general. You cannot change the past, so there is little sense in thinking about your regrets other than to learn from them.

Regardless of the specific cause of your low confidence, remember that they all lead to the same place – a downward spiral. You only need to hear one word that triggers you to feel bad about yourself, and this can lead to a chain reaction that erodes your confidence.

Focus instead on what is possible. Focus instead on the fact that if you choose to impose your personal will on your personal reality today, things can happen. That's what confidence can do for you.

This all involves a high level of introspection. This all involves a high level of personal honesty. Which of the above apply to you? When did they happen and were you actually at fault? You need to be emotionally authentic and be prepared to sacrifice a lot of emotional safe harbors to get clarify on why exactly you might feel the way that you do about yourself.

Law 4. Recognize and defeat imposter syndrome.

Last week I met someone who had 4 degrees that I can remember and was fabulously accomplished in life. I engaged them in deep conversation, and walked away with the startling realization that that person didn't identify with their accomplishments, and lived under the constant belief that they didn't deserve their station in life.

They didn't feel like a loser, but they felt like they didn't truly belong, and everything in their life was a façade for the lesser and truer version of themselves. Like they had tricked everyone in their professional life to get where they were.

This is the more common way that **imposter syndrome** rears its ugly head. No matter how accomplished you might be, and how many people would kill to be in the same position as you... there is a shocking difference in that person's self-perception.

Imposter syndrome describes a personality trait where a person still feels like a **fraud or imposter** despite a wealth of information and facts to the contrary. They feel like they are don't quite fit in, and don't deserve the position or power they have achieved. In fact, the more money, power, and respect this person gets, the smaller they feel. This is the **paradox of the imposter syndrome.**

People with this syndrome feel that whatever the accomplishments that they have achieved in life are simply the result of **luck**, somebody handing it to them, or some sort of mass delusion regarding their own particular level of competence. The conclusion is always the same: they don't deserve the success that they have.

The reality, however, is that the imposter syndrome affects everyone. It affects everyone at some level and at some point in his or her lives, and can be a major detractor to your confidence – another confidence drainer.

The immediate impact of the imposter syndrome is that it erodes your confidence. You feel small. You feel insignificant. You feel powerless.

But your external reality is very different. People would love to live in your house, drive your car, have your bank account, or travel the world like you do. But when it comes to your perspective, you feel that it isn't enough. It is not good enough. You are the biggest loser among your friends.

This disparity between your expectations and your personal mental picture of your life, can only lead to lower levels of confidence.

The main reason why the imposter syndrome is so prevalent is that we are **slaves of our own expectations**. We expect so much out of ourselves that we end up setting such a high bar that regardless of how far we outpace everyone else, we still feel like giant losers because we can't seem to get close to the bar we set for ourselves.

By judging ourselves using impossibly high bars of achievement or quality, we risk triggering a downward spiral. If you question your ability to assert control over your personal reality and to take care of business, it can lead to disastrous consequences to your confidence. Worst of all, it can become a **self-fulfilling prophecy**.

For example, if you feel resigned that you aren't good at your career, then you won't be pushing yourself to excel and succeed. You'll start believing that fact, and settle for less than stellar work. You'll produce mediocre work that is uninspired and unmotivated. Instead of motivating you, the phrase "*I am not good enough*" becomes a self-fulfilling reality.

Other people eventually catch on and this impacts your career or business or social standing. Not surprisingly, everything you've worked so hard for in the past falls apart.

Breaking free of the imposter syndrome is not easy. Above all else, the imposter syndrome is a **mental habit**. It may have worked for us in the past, or it may be currently working for us because it produces positive results. People don't hang on to habits if they don't get something out of those habits.

Unfortunately, this type of mental syndrome is **toxic** and you pay with your confidence and self-esteem.

Instead of looking inwards towards your skewed self-perception, look at the achievements of other people and use them as **benchmarks for your success**.

You don't have to beat yourself up to take yourself to the next level. You don't have to degrade your perception of your capability, your personality, or even your personal self-worth just so you can get ahead.

In many cases, you have to sacrifice a lot of your sacred cows so you can be fully free of the imposter syndrome. You must sacrifice the very comforting thought that things are not good enough, or that there is a better level. You have to let go of the fear that if you start appreciating your accomplishments, you would start to stagnate.

Feel free to pat yourself on the back. Eventually, you should start focusing on objective third party standards of accomplishments so you can go to where you need to go.

Law 5. Draw confidence internally.

Who doesn't like being patted on the back? (Or head, if you're a dog.)

Positive encouragement is enough to make our day sometimes, and it tells us that we are doing a good job and headed in the right direction. A standing ovation can be the highlight of a person's entire life.

However, a problem arises if you become dependent on such outside gratification to prop up your confidence and self-esteem. It's a dangerous position to be in when you are depending on sources other than yourself to make yourself feel good strong and confident.

This is very reminiscent of **Niccolo Machiavelli's** celebrated book, *The Prince*. In it, he states that it is far better and more effective to be feared than loved.

How does that apply here? There are better and more helpful emotions to receive from others than simple love and admiration. If you receive purely love and admiration, you can imagine how damaging to your perception and worldview that can be. And if suddenly that love and admiration from external sources was removed, how lost you might feel.

Confidence built by others is a losing proposition.

The only winning proposition is to build your confidence and self-esteem internally – this way, you are always in control.

If your source of energy and power comes from other people, what happens if, for some reason or another, it gets cut off? Chances are you will suffer and fall apart. Wither away without your source of strength like Superman cut off from the sun.

When you are fueled from external sources, you will eventually meet a challenging situation where you will fail because your external sources can't continually provide you with the energy and confidence that you need.

The only person you really can depend on is you, and if you depend on other people you leave yourself incredibly vulnerable – and not in the positive way I subscribe to later in this book. You simply put yourself at their mercy and at their control. This is hardly a recipe for success.

The only person you can depend on is yourself. This will allow you solely to control your levels of happiness and confidence. Stop trying to gain these from others, because eventually, they have to take care of themselves and let you down in some fashion – because they are their own first priorities as well! Eventually, they will stop the supply to you so they can have more of it for themselves. What happens to you then?

True confidence must come from within. If you base your confidence on other people, you are relying on a power source that can be cut off at any time.

When you base your confidence on how other people think of you, you will find yourself high and dry when those people move on or focus on someone else. You obviously can't control those people so you need to get your confidence from the validation of the one person you have most control over – yourself.

You will fail sometimes. You let other people down from time to time. What makes you think that they wouldn't let you down, even if you they say they won't? You have to support yourself 100%.

Instead of trying to get the respect, admiration and affirmation from other people, learn to respect yourself. Build your base from within. Learn to love yourself more and expect better results from yourself. As long as you don't let yourself down, which you won't, you are in a great position.

Law 6. Catalog your strengths and ACTUAL weaknesses.

This chapter was titled very carefully.

ACTUAL weaknesses. What's the significance of that?

When people with low confidence try to come up with things they are good at, the list is usually pitifully short. People are far too hard on themselves, and have a difficult time realizing what they are ACTUALLY good or bad at. In many cases, these weaknesses are imagined, and the strengths marginalized or rationalized.

These weaknesses are more of a reflection of their fear of rejection and past bad experiences rather than of reality. It turns out that many of our perceived 'weaknesses' aren't actually weaknesses.

If you want to truly boost your confidence, you have to ground your perception of your weaknesses in hard reality.

So get out a sheet of paper and actually write out what you feel that you are better than many other people at, and what you are worse at. Focus on your **true** strengths and your **actual** weaknesses. The whole point of this exercise is to discover how you actually perceive yourself. You can discover if you have a low mental picture of yourself, and work to correct that. If you have a low mental picture of yourself, what you are capable of doing, and your self-worth, it is very easy to feel powerless and unconfident.

It will be easy to tell where you fall on the spectrum because your list of weaknesses will be far longer than your list of strengths and talents. In fact, make it a goal to have the lists be equal in length – for every weakness, list a strength to make sure that you are accurately describing yourself.

When you interact with other people, they will absolutely detect this low level of confidence and in some cases even exploit it. If you don't want to be taken advantage of or dismissed, you need to project the right level of confidence.

The best way to do this is to catalog your strengths and actual weaknesses. By getting a realistic view of what you are capable of doing, you can base your confidence level on what is real instead of what you fear or what you imagine.

The great thing about listing down your personal strengths is that you are getting a clear picture of the things that you should be proud about. We all have an ability, trait, or habit that they can be proud and confident about, maybe that we're the best in the world at even. It can be as silly as twisting your tongue or finding parking spaces, but they are all valid talents that give you value.

There will always be something positive about you. You will spot something positive if you look hard enough, and you can hold onto that in hard times. What is it that you can do well? What is it that you can offer to other people? More than you might think.

Everyone obviously has weaknesses and things that they need improvement on. If you are really honest with yourself and devoid of denial, you'll know exactly what yours are.

Most people's greatest challenge is their attitude towards these negative elements. Just like an ostrich is not going to make a lion go away when it buries its head in the sand, simply denying that you have weaknesses is not going to make them go away.

In order to tackle your weaknesses and possibly turn them into positive traits later on, you have to get rid of **coping mechanisms** that may have proved so useful in the past to protect yourself. No excuses are allowed. A high level of emotional discipline, authenticity and honesty is needed at this point to make real progress.

Regardless of how many people in the past called you lazy, dumb or stupid, focus on the fact that you do indeed have strengths and talents and have managed great accomplishments in the past. This is crucial to getting the level of confidence you need about the positive elements in your life for you to make real progress in establishing a realistic confidence level.

If you want to increase your confidence level, focus on your accomplishments. Track them. Track what you don't do well, and realize that **you have your own talents regardless**. See how you can take them to the next level so you can get even more confidence from the things that you truly do well.

Law 7. Perfection is an utter myth.

To many, **Bill Gates** represents perfection. Yet he isn't handsome.

And to others, a **Brazilian swimsuit model** represents perfection. Yet you might assume that she isn't intelligent.

One of the worst reasons why people have low self-confidence is that they think that they have to be perfect to feel good about themselves. If they can't meet this magical standard, they are worthless or they are worth less compared to other people. If this is how you think, you are just beating yourself up unnecessarily. You are chasing after ghosts that even Bill Gates or Gisele Bundchen cannot fulfill.

You are running after something that doesn't exist.

Perfection is a complete and utter myth. Everybody has flaws. Everybody has weaknesses. Everything has chinks in their armor. There is no such thing as a person who offers only strengths and has no weaknesses whatsoever.

This is what makes us human. Our flaws, warts, flaws, and blemishes are what keep us real-and lovable. People bond over their flaws. They don't bond based on how close they are to an imagined idea.

If you are trying to live your life for the myth of perfection, you are playing the game of life to fail. By wasting your time and precious energy chasing after something that doesn't exist and letting it play with your emotions, you are simply wasting your life.

Yes, you are flawed... and so is everyone else.

Accept this fact. Live with it. Be okay with it. The reality is that you fall far short of the standard... and so does everyone else. Why should you beat yourself up about your imperfection when most everyone else is more than happy to get on with life?

The perfect ideal exists only in our minds and is only as real as we permit it to be. While it is one thing to strive for ambitious ideals, it is another thing to allow yourself to feel miserable when you fall far short of the mark.

You are not perfect, and that is perfectly acceptable.
By being clear on this central fact, you can then start
moving forward.

What this means is that when you look at perfection,
you don't look at it as something that is attainable but
more like **a helpful road sign**. It just points you in the
right direction and tells you that you are heading
there. That's the purpose of having a perfect ideal.

Compare this with beating yourself up if you don't
produce a specific or exact result that you consider
perfect. Instead, **perfection is just part of the process
instead of the destination.**

Confidence is all about knowing your flaws and
owning them, and knowing your limitations. What
separates confident people from not-so-confident
people is that you are perfectly happy with your flaws.
You've worked hard to fix them but you know the
limitations they have and how far they can go. After a
certain point, you are at peace with your flaws.

The people who lack confidence, on the other hand,
either deny their flaws, run away from their flaws, or
otherwise feel bad about their flaws. Not surprisingly,
they let their flaws and imperfections own them.

This leads to a downward spiral of not feeling good enough, not meeting some arbitrary standard, and beating yourself up emotionally and mentally over something that you cannot control. To make matters worse, other people can more easily take advantage of people who have low confidence due to their perfectionism.

By understanding that there is no such thing as a perfect person, you place everybody in the same boat. When nobody can meet that imaginary standard, you shouldn't feel the pressure of being the person who would meet the standard.

Instead, enjoy the journey of life within the bounds of realistic milestones that are bound to fulfill you more. **Life is a process instead of a set of fixed results as perfection dictates.**

Law 8. Vulnerability displays supreme confidence.

How does acknowledging your vulnerabilities and sharing them with others build your confidence? It seems so counter-intuitive.

Wouldn't you come off as more confident if you hid your vulnerabilities and weaknesses from other people? Appear invincible?

Well, **no**.

It's too easy to fall into the trap of overcompensation, too much pride, and hubris if you don't allow yourself to show any weaknesses. We all know people that fit this description, and they are usually **insufferable know-it-alls**.

Interestingly enough, the more open you are about your weaknesses and limitations, the more positively people will view you, and the better you will feel about yourself.

Vulnerability is a concept that you should embrace fully because of what it represents about you, and consequently how people will perceive you. Your vulnerability, ability to accept it, acknowledge it, and share it with others will make you a **magnetic force**.

As much as we like the idea of perfection, it is our imperfections that draw us to each other. It makes us human and it makes us relatable as people. It wouldn't be a stretch to say that your vulnerability might be your **greatest gift**.

And as it relates to confidence, showing your vulnerability and owning up to your flaws displays the most supreme version of it.

Let's look at our friend the **peacock** for a moment.

He is one of the most unique creatures in the world. As you probably know, the male peacock has a very long and elaborate tail that is the opposite of practical. It limits his ability to run fast, and makes him practically a bulls-eye for predators.
It would be an understatement to say that the male peacock's tail is a liability, vulnerability.

But that flashy tail serves another important purpose in the male peacock's life – to confidently show his presence and virility to females. **So on one hand, the**

tail is a sign of vulnerability, and on the other hand a display of supreme confidence.

Something that would literally kill the male peacock actually increases the likelihood that he will pass his genes on to the next generation.

There are very clear parallels to the relationship between confidence and vulnerability in humans.

The more confident you are about your shortcomings, the more people are drawn to you. It shows to people that you have things well enough under control that you can be public about your weaknesses. You must have a deep reserve of strength and personal power that people will both admire and respect. In the same way the male peacock appears strong and confident to female peacocks, **when you admit your shortcomings, people are more willing to respect and admire you.**

On the other hand, when you are uncomfortable with your flaws and attempt to cover them up in various ways, you make other people uncomfortable as well as question your integrity.

Simply, when you are comfortable with your weaknesses, it shows strength. The reason why this paradox exists is because **it sets you apart from everybody else**.

Everybody else wants to put on a show that they don't have these weaknesses and limitations. No one ever buys this act because we all know deep inside that it can't be true. Everyone has flaws and to pretend otherwise is dishonest and insecure.

If you step out from the herd and admit that you have these weaknesses, it makes you look strong, honest, and in control of who you are. People are more likely to respect and admire you because you essentially say what other people are afraid to admit.

By admitting your limitations, you also enable others to step up and admit their own limitations. They may not verbalize them to you, but they admit it by being open to you. And by you being open, they feel like they know you. **They feel that there is an emotional and personal gateway** that has been between you and them simply based on the fact that you owned up to your weaknesses.

For example, admitting that you have a drinking problem can open up to you other people who are suffering from addiction issues. And on a personal note, I can't tell you how many people have opened up to me about their various insecurities and vulnerabilities after I tell them I was a **fat kid**. I don't wield that fact for that purpose, but it's always a natural instinct after they learn about it.

Finally, vulnerability is quite **beautiful to share with others**.

When you share your vulnerability, you open yourself up to other people and they are drawn to open themselves up to you. People with the same interest like to share. They like to hang out with each other. **They feel they are not alone**. They feel that in whatever trials they are going through, they don't have to go through alone.

You start the process by opening up and admitting to your vulnerability. This makes you instantly more likeable. This should boost your confidence because, at the end of the day, you are not alone. People are drawn and attracted to you because of your limitations instead of your pretensions of perfection.

Law 9. Choose to be confident on a daily basis.

One of the most crippling myths about building unshakeable confidence and overcoming insecurities is the idea that you have to reinvent yourself – change in profound ways such that your newfound confidence may then be seen and reflected.

There's nothing fundamentally wrong with this idea because it has only the best intentions.

I've said time and time again that true confidence must be rooted from within, and arrived at after objective introspection. However, **confidence as a process is a long-term goal and takes practice**. Everyone can agree to this and subscribe to it, but not everyone can live up to it, so what's the more practical and interim approach to building your confidence?

The best practical and interim strategy to building confidence is by making confidence a choice every day. Intentionally and consciously choose to act

confident and embody confident mindsets on a daily basis. In other words, start acting confident to become confident.

If you want to start building your confidence, you have to **outwardly project** the confidence that you may lack in reality.

Of course, this highlights the fact that the process of confidence can start internally or externally… but **both aspects must be present for true confidence.**

Some might recognize this strategy as being relatively similar to *"faking it 'til you make it,"* but I shy away from using that phrase for a few reasons. In fact, I hate that phrase. **First**, I feel that it is reductive and unhelpful for most people. It's like telling someone to get better at surfing by surfing better. **Second**, it doesn't actually solve root problems and just attempts to address symptoms. **Finally**, it's a solution that won't work for most people because they simply won't be able to do it. They will still have mental blocks that they won't be able to break through.

So you might question yourself, which is natural. You might have low self-esteem, or feel that everyone in the room has more to offer than you. None of that matters – **what matters is how others perceive your level of confidence**. This might sound counterintuitive, because the root of confidence shouldn't depend on other people. But it's not simply a matter of depending on others – it's taking advantage of the signals and feedback that people will give you.

When you act confidently, people will treat you like a confident person and send you the signals of respect and admiration you've been looking for, which triggers a cycle of feeling good about yourself and rising confidence. It all leads to an upward spiral.

This is a choice that you can trigger on a daily basis; **you have to make the first move**. It's all about sending off the right signals, going through the right rituals, and projecting the right level of confidence so that a chain reaction can take place.

Eventually, this process allows you to stop consciously making that choice because your confidence level would have risen naturally as a result of the feedback you got from others.

Up until that time, you still have to **prime the pump** by taking the first step and making that choice.

Underlying this whole strategy is the fact that confidence is always a choice. If you feel bad about yourself and limited regarding what you're capable of doing, guess what? **You chose to feel that way and you could just as easily choose to feel differently.**

People who are overtly negative, and people who let their lives defeat them always choose to look at the glass half-empty. **It's like being trapped in a prison cell with the key in your hand.** You can always step out of your mental prison whenever you want. Unfortunately, it has become so comfortable that you'd rather stay miserable inside.

Positivity and confidence go hand in hand. It is very hard to find very positive people who are not confident. If you are not confident that things will turn out well or that things can and will be better, how can you be positive? Similarly, how can you look at the best things in life if you feel that you're not really in control?

The best way to nurture positivity is to, once again, make a conscious choice to embody it. Your external actions can give you the feedback that you need to become more positive to project more confidence.

When you look at where you've been, the hurdles that you have conquered, and the challenges that you have overcome, you will realize that things aren't so bad. You will realize that as much as your ultimate goal is still a long distance away, you've made quite a great deal of progress.

Perspective is crucial to nurturing positivity. Without it, you will always feel that your back is to the wall and the only way to go is down.

But making the choice to control your perspective and outlook on positivity will make the world of difference in building your confidence. **All it takes is a deep breath each morning as you look at yourself in the morning, and deciding that you will be the person you want to be that day.**

Law 10. Preparation guarantees confidence.

It's perfectly fine to have low confidence.

First of all, you are hardly alone. We all have our shortcomings; none of us are perfect. **We are all works in progress**.

Second, self-confidence is learned. Just take a look at the introduction of this book for the prime example of how confidence is not innate – me.

As I covered in the previous chapter, there are a series of shortcuts and hacks that can speed up your trajectory towards confidence. There are ways that you can learn to feel like you're always in control and on top of any situation you find yourself in. This chapter details another one.

Let's just imagine a situation that you might not be entirely comfortable or confident in. **A speech in front of a large crowd**, perhaps.

You innately know that to feel better and more confident for your speech, you would need to spend hours preparing and practicing in front of a mirror to make sure that you present exactly how you want.

So why hasn't this mindset made the leap into other areas of your life?

If you are suffering from low levels of confidence at work or in your social life, you can overcome it with a bit of preparation and planning.

If you were to honestly ask yourself why you feel a lack of confidence regarding particular things in your life, you'd come to one answer: lack of control. You are uncertain about many things because you feel that you can't get the kind of results that you are looking for, and you feel that the power is out of your hands. **The outcomes are unpredictable**.

Now what if you could make things predictable?

What if you could do things in such a way that the outcomes you were expecting turned out time and time again? Wouldn't you feel better about yourself? Wouldn't you feel more confident? This is precisely what happens when you prepare and plan for the things that you normally do that tend to erode your confidence.

For example, if you have a tough time making presentations in front of large groups of people, you might be feeling this way because you tend to drop the ball, you tend to make a fool out of yourself by embarrassingly stumbling over your words.

Isn't that something that you can prepare for relatively adequately? What if you could practice to ensure that you could pull off a smooth and flawless presentation? Wouldn't doing this repeatedly change your overall perception of making public presentations? You know it would. Moreover, wouldn't this be a huge boon and boost to your confidence? This is why making things as predictable as possible helps boost your confidence.

When you do a lot of planning, and you do a lot of dress rehearsals, and you keep honing your skills, you reduce the likelihood of committing errors. You increase the likelihood that you will pull things off perfectly. The more you achieve a smooth, drama-free and predictable execution, the higher your confidence becomes.

If you want to be confident in any kind of skill or any area of your life, just focus on one thing: repetition. The more you do something again and again, in different contexts, the better you get at it.

It really is all about learning from your mistakes and using your native intelligence to come up with better, more efficient and faster ways to do something. Eventually, you will be able to hone your skills to a higher level that you can do it in your sleep. This will have a tremendously positive impact on your confidence level.

When you feel that you can predictably do something without much thinking, it's easy to become confident at it.

When you plan ahead of time, you are able to focus on the things that will make a really big difference. Once you are able to execute something as smoothly as possible, you can feel confident about the results. **This also allows you to focus on smaller aspects of your performance that will make a difference, if you can remove yourself from worrying about simply not flopping.** You won't need to focus on just getting by – you can focus on really knocking something out of the park, which will further increase your levels of confidence.

You only need to repeat this a few times for your confidence to improve. Eventually, if you apply this principle to a wide number of areas in your life, you can achieve a high level of overall confidence.

You have a lot more control over your confidence than you give yourself credit for. Confidence can be built through repetition. It's all about gaining the correct appreciation and right level of comfort with your skill level in all areas of your life.

You don't have to gain confidence through trial by fire. You can, through planning, leisurely and systematically work on your confidence level.

Law 11. Run towards failure.

Ah, failure. He who shall not be named, and he who shall be avoided at any cost possible.

What about embracing and running towards failure?

This may sound counterintuitive, but failure is one of the best things that can happen to us. Failure is one of the best teachers you will ever have in your life, and its value will far exceed any successes you have.

We successfully learn what not to do when we fail. Sadly, when we spend so much time and energy trying to evade and avoid failure, we end up learning those hard lessons later on. Instead of trying to avoid failure, look at it straight in the eye, learn what you need to learn and move on. This fundamental truth is especially important when it comes to your confidence.

Instead of constantly trying to run **from** failure, try running **to** failure.

If you know that failure is headed your way, instead of wasting all that time, energy and motivation trying to escape its clutches, why don't you just turn around, look at it in the eye and embrace it to see what you can learn about yourself from it? Don't spend your time trying to stay afloat just to avoid failure. That just leads to half-measures, and won't teach you much about yourself.

Meticulously pick apart why you failed in a specific social situation, and exactly what caused your confidence to tank or otherwise not rise. Attempt to understand what you did wrong, what you did right, and what was special regarding the situation. **You can then use this information so you can avoid making that same mistake in the future**.

Pay attention to things like the topics of your discussions, your mannerisms and gestures, your tone of voice, who was around you at the time, your timing, and many other factors. **Come up with a pattern**. Come up with a theory of why things fell apart and what the solution is. Test your solution by practicing again and again with other groups of people.

Life is a big test. We are constantly getting opportunities to learn what we did right and build on them, as well as recognize the things that we did wrong and avoid doing them in the future. By embracing failure, and divorcing it from the feelings of alienation, regret, shame, and embarrassment, and appreciating it for its learning opportunities, we can make great progress.

We can to increase our level of self-confidence by resolving to become better students of failure.

Failure exists as a sign. It's a sign that something did not go right.

It's emotionally neutral.

However, human beings have been programmed since early on to read all sorts of mental and emotional judgments into failure. Just because you failed doesn't mean you are less of a person. Don't give yourself permission to feel miserable about your failures. Don't let failure lead to an emotional shutdown that gives you anxiety or frustrated you. Instead, look at failure as a set of signals that something didn't go wrong... a blueprint to exactly how to succeed and seize confidence. If it did not destroy you, it has only made you stronger if you allow it to.

The problem with success is that you don't know which part of the particular experience produced the positive result. It's easy to go about things with a false sense of security when success comes easily to you. It's a problem of correlation with causation.

With failure, it's much easier to break apart your actions and understand the patterns that lead disappointment, discouragement and frustration. Since things are easier to pick apart and understand, it's much easier to improve when you are faced with failure. **Failure can be a stepping-stone to greater success if you let it fulfill that role.**

Your level of confidence is a reflection of your relationship with failure and fear.

Most people are so afraid of failure that it erodes their level of confidence. This really is a tragedy because if you choose to learn from failure, and you avoid making the same mistakes in the future, you can actually gain confidence. Failure can in fact make you a more confident person because you learn about the signals and the data, and the feedback that you need to become a better person, make better decisions, and improve your situation.

Instead of failure sucking up all your energy, or converting your energy to negative energy, redirect that energy. Instead feeling apprehensive, embarrassed, or otherwise negative about failure, look at it as a positive development.

Look at it as something you look forward to. **Look at it as stepping into a classroom and being handed a very valuable textbook**. When you do this, your whole set of expectations and assumptions about failure changes, and you are able to extract more wisdom, and understanding, and life lessons from your failures.

Learn to respect and appreciate failure, and you will be rewarded with better insights that would lead to greater successes and confidence in the future.

Law 12. Practice confidence to gain it.

In an ideal world, we would all possess the internal confidence to jumpstart and project our external confidence.

Of course, confidence as the process that I've described inherently takes a while and is easier said than done. I've covered a few confidence hacks by which you can jumpstart the road the true confidence, and **practicing confidence in small doses on a daily basis is another one**.

This is again premised on the upward spirals created by the feedback you get from other people reacting to your confident presence. Make first move and the decision to practice confidence.

Specifically, **by practicing confidence in small areas of your life, you set yourself up with a confidence that can translate to bigger areas of your life**. Starting small allows you to take baby steps to gain the level of confidence you need to start making real and effective changes in major areas of your life.

It also involves changes in your behavior, and more importantly your expectations, assumptions, and mindset.

Always keep in mind that **if your mindset doesn't change, nothing will be possible**. You will feel stuck, that there is no way to improve your situation, and that happiness is impossible. However, if you open yourself to the possibility of improvement through small steps and intimate settings, you can set a process in motion that can scale up with time.

It's all about making that decision to start the process. It's all about resolving to stare your confidence problems in the eye and heading in that direction, instead of turning around and running away.

So what are eight ways you can practice confidence on a daily basis?

First, assume that you have what it takes. Even if you feel that you know that you might not have what it takes, assume you have what it takes. You will surprise yourself on a daily basis. This establishes the base with which your confidence will rest. Assume that things are doable; you will be that much more likely to accomplish them and your confidence.

Second, assume that you are good enough. Look at yourself in the mirror, and say to yourself you are good enough to do this. If you repeat it enough times, you start to believe it. Don't let negative mindsets creep into your life.

Third, start taking slow actions. As mentioned in the examples in this book, start small. Start taking daily actions. Build upon them and gather momentum to your ultimate goals.

Fourth, repetition. Keep repeating and practicing the same action day in, day out. The more you do something, the more comfortable you become, and the better you get at it. And of course, the more confident you become in yourself.

Fifth, let the power of momentum move you forward. By constantly doing things that you normally be afraid of doing, or have a low amount of confidence doing, you let momentum take over. It will take a life of its own because you continuously do it, and you will be able to scale up. You will have a far higher baseline of confidence and courage to work with every day.

Six, scale up the challenge. Now that you have achieved the sense of momentum, keep scaling up every day. Challenge yourself every day with greater heights. Try to explore new things in the area that you're trying to get confidence about. You may not succeed all the time, but accomplishment isn't the goal here.

Seventh, go for a home run daily. At one point in your day, try to do the impossible. Try to sell a big-ticket item or try to meet that attractive member of the opposite sex. Whatever the big challenge is, always set up one instance where you basically try to take a moonshot. Nine times out of ten, you may fail, but it doesn't matter. What's important is that you take that shot. Once you hit the home run, it will skyrocket your confidence. You will also find that the worst-case scenario of failing isn't as bad as you might think it is, and that the failure can teach you numerous things.

Eighth and finally, track your progress. Regardless of what you do to practice your confidence on a daily basis, make sure you keep a journal. This will enable you to track the progress you're making and how far you've come from the beginning. By having a clear written record, you can see how far you've come, and how to improve what you're doing so you can scale up properly. Most importantly, it will give you perspective of your improvement, which should boost your confidence as well.

Law 13. Incremental goals stack confidence.

A high level of confidence is not going to magically drop on your lap. You can't just read a book on confidence (*even this one!*) and have your life suddenly transform with confidence. Confidence is something that you have to work for and seize for yourself.

If you're tired of hoping and wishing for better results, you can start getting better results by setting **incremental confidence goals**.

Setting goals is much better than simply hoping and wishing because **goals focus on action**. Goals require you to set up a sequence of steps you need to take, within a timeline, to make something happen by action.

Hopes and wishes on the other hand simply involve you sitting back and imagining how things could be if certain other things took place. **Hopes and wishes**

leave you waiting and frustrated while goals kick your life into gear.

Just as it's possible to get from point A to point B by simply putting one foot in front of the other, you can get to a high level of confidence by simply setting the right goals. All goals are achievable if you break them up into **small enough pieces**. If you put the right kind of timeline on them and you actually put the time, effort, and energy into each sub-goal, you will be surprised as to the kind of things you can achieve.

Start with small goals.

If you are afraid of the opposite sex, if you are afraid of speaking to a large crowd of people, nothing will freak you out more than stepping up to the podium. If you do things this way, you're starting out with very big goals. **You're starting out with the end objective.**

Obviously, you're going to fail. You set yourself up for failure. You fear these situations and if these are your goals from the outset, chances are you'll fail because you are inadequately prepared for them.

Instead, start with small goals. If you are afraid of talking to a large group of people, you can break down that goal into talking in front of one person. Make it your goal to become truly confident in front of that person. Study your interaction and dynamics very carefully. Figure out what patterns or techniques you can apply when you talk to two people.

Next, talk to two people. Again, figure out what works and what doesn't work. Practice again until you are very comfortable and confident dealing with two people. Keep scaling up by following the pattern described above. Pretty soon, you'll find yourself interacting with huge amounts of people without breaking a sweat.

Incremental increase is the key to success.

As mentioned above, one way to overcome fear of public speaking is to start with very small crowds. The smallest crowd is, of course, yourself. Look at the mirror, and talk to yourself. Once you become comfortable talking to yourself, increase the crowd size by one.

Measure how you feel when you're talking. Look at your strong points, and fix your weak spots. Once you've made some adjustments, make an incremental increase and ask another friend to listen to your speeches. Now you have a crowd of two. Keep repeating this process until you have a fairly large crowd.

Incremental increases don't really fundamentally change your skill set. What they do impact is your sense of confidence. The good news is the better you get at something, the more confident you become, and the easier the next step will be.

The step by step process with setting goals is pretty straightforward.

First, you need to take a big goal, and then break it up into small parts. The break up can be in terms of scale. If your ultimate goal is to deliver a speech in front of one thousand people, you should start with one person. And then two people, then maybe five people, and then ten people. And then scale up with time.

Your goal should not be necessarily the number of people, but the feeling that you get when talking to those people. And most importantly, the sense of possibility you achieve when you accomplish scaling up from a crowd of five people, to fifteen, to fifty, and to one hundred people. Let this positive feeling get the best of you. Own it. Savor it. Don't feel that you just got lucky, don't feel that you're just setting yourself up for failure.

Instead savor the distinct experience of looking your fear in the eye, confronting it head-on, and beating it.

That is the ultimate feeling that you should be looking for because that's the base your confidence should be built on.

Law 14. Look good to feel good.

This principle is simple.

When you look and project yourself a certain way, you eventually become that way.

If you want to be confident, you have to look confident. You have to physically have the image of a confident person.

The reason this works is not because of *'faking it 'til you make it,'* but because we look at certain signals from the outside world, and configure our realities accordingly. This is why when people treat you with respect and admiration, you start developing a deep and profound sense of self-confidence. The more confident you become, the more they respect you. The more they respect you, the more confident you become. And you ride this upward spiral to a deep and profound sense of self-confidence and self-worth.

This process can actually be triggered simply by how you choose to dress and present yourself physically. Your grooming, your physical appearance, your facial expressions, the clothes you wear, the accessories you buy, the car you drive – all these can combine to give you a physical image that sends your subconscious the signals that would trigger an escalating process that leads to a higher level of self-confidence. **Overhauling your physical image is an essential step to confidence.**

We've all seen those makeover television shows where they take someone that dresses like a bum, and completely transforms them physically. The real transformation isn't just in the appearance of that person. That person, if he or she wanted to, could take a shower, get a haircut, and buy the right clothes.

Instead, the person chose to believe certain assumptions stemming from their physical image that leads nowhere positive. If you change your physical appearance, you can change your internal level of confidence.

If you want to embark on a confidence makeover, your first stop should be the gym. Start with baby steps. Consistently to go to the gym or be active in some regard. The key is to start enjoying physical changes with your body. When you perceive that you have achieved a better shape, you feel better about yourself. If you feel that you have become fitter, the way you look at yourself changes. Your clothes will fit differently, and you'll notice the opposite sex checking you out more. All of this contributes to confidence.

Second, improve your wardrobe. This may not be something you've ever given much thought to, but there are reasons that businessmen and salespeople dress the way that they do. There are certain clothes and accessories that send signals to other people.

At the very least, your clothing and your wardrobe make people take you more seriously or appear more attractive. In other cases, they make people pay more attention to you. **If you are driving a Toyota Tercel, you are getting a certain level of attention**. Now what if you are driving a Ferrari? You probably will get a different level and kind of attention.

The clothes you wear, the accessories you buy, the car you drive, all these are like costumes or masks and allow you to tap into certain responses based on what you choose. If you want to be respected, dress the way a respected and attractive person dresses. If you want to make sales, dress the way a power salesperson would dress. If you're stuck on this point, grab a friend of the opposite sex and go to the mall!

It's as easy as asking for help once, and it will pay invaluable dividends afterwards.

Some of the tips in this chapter might seem fake, disingenuous or fraudulent to you. Well, the reality is the world is shallow. That's the world we live in.

Since people are fake, shallow, and judge books by their covers, you should do the same and play the game accordingly. There's no sense in willfully denying the game if you aren't getting the kind of results that you want.

Once you get the right kind of signals, you can become more confident and this can start the whole chain reaction where you eventually end up with true internal self-confidence.

Law 15. Physical acts create physiological confidence.

The body and mind are connected in funny ways, and they aren't all completely understood yet.

You can literally make body believe something and react accordingly just be thinking it. Just take the **placebo effect**, for example.

Is it scientific? At best, we can answer "sort of." Sometimes the effects are undeniable, and it's a sign of mind over matter and the power of our belief.

It's a relief to know that the opposite path – body changing mind – is also a pathway that works. This is obviously great for your confidence, because it means that you can start with external changes that produce internal mindset shifts. In other words, **what your body does can make your mind follow.**

Confidence as a process can be painstaking, so it's about time that we take advantage of our physiologically to help develop our confidence.

Put simply, you need to start acting confident so you can feel confident inside. You can turn this into a set of daily physical rituals, because it's been scientifically proven that physical actions promote physiological changes that match the mindsets that you want to aspire to.

Beyond that, it's also a great habit to get into of acting outwardly confident, so even if you're feeling blue, you won't appear to do so and others will give you the positive feedback that is so important to developing your confidence.

Remember, when you act confident, people will perceive you as confident. At the end of the process, you can become a truly confident person both inside and out. You can jumpstart this process by simply utilizing confident actions on a daily basis.

First of all, speak slowly and deliberately.

When you speak slowly and deliberately, you send a message to other people that you mean business. When you choose your language carefully and avoid any kind of weak language, hedging, or non-committal language, you stand out from the crowd. The reality is that everybody is so afraid of offending other people that we limit ourselves, we engage in gray-area language that doesn't really do anybody any favors. At the very least, it doesn't make us look confident, decisive, or all that smart.

The best way to speak confidently is to channel someone you know is confident. If you know a political leader who is decisive, firm, and important, you can always choose to pretend to speak like them. Ask yourself, what would they say in a particular situation? How would they position themselves? When you channel that person, you tap into the confidence level and power of their words.

Second, harness strong posture.

Your words carry more weight when you are sending physical signals along with it. Actually, studies have shown that body language and posture account for more of the message we send than the words that come out of our mouths.

People are always looking for leaders.

They would like to believe that they are leading themselves, and are self-confident. But in reality, they want the decisions made for them. This is why when you go into any kind of social setting, there's always a couple of people who are working that room. They do this with their body language and overall presence —

everyone else falls into line and lets them fulfill the role of the leader of that situation.

If you want to be such a leader, tilt your head up, stick your chest out, point your thumbs up, cross your arms in a confident way, put your hands on your waist, and stand straight up (not all at once, of course). These postures and body language signals send a clear message to other people in the room that you are important, that you are to be taken seriously. When they respond favorably, your confidence level grows, and you're able to send more of the same types of power signals.

Third, use power gestures and poses.

When you gesture, it means that you believe in what you are doing. This can be interpreted as a sign of confidence and conviction. Normally, people like to keep their vulnerability close to their chests. They like to hide their vulnerabilities. This means they protect their chests and torsos with small gestures that don't capture a lot of attention. They're afraid.

However, when you gesture, you're opening yourself up and increasing the size of your presence. This means that you must use big, strong, confident power gestures, as opposed to small gestures that hint at your insecurities.

Power gestures give the impression of someone that knows exactly what they are saying and trying to convey, while small, hesitant gestures make someone appear unsure. If you do a gesture only halfway, people will think that you are only halfway sure of what you are saying. Power gestures require committing to the words coming out of your mouth, as well as your gesture. Embrace this and watch as your persuasion and charm over others increases immediately.

Remember, the mind can follow the body, so lead with confidence and strength.

16. Eleven simple confidence hacks.

One of the main reasons why confidence is so rare nowadays is because people think it is a big project. People make confidence out to be some sort of Holy Grail that they have to go through all sorts of challenges and hardships to get.

Confidence is as easy you allow it to be. If you want to gain confidence, there are many easy ways to do so. You don't need to pay a steep price, you don't need to subject yourself to all sorts of trials by fire. In fact, you only need to do eleven simple things to gain confidence in a systematic and methodical way.

1. Always be thankful.

The first step to gaining self-confidence is to be thankful for being yourself. This may seem ridiculous because people with low confidence aren't exactly thankful for being who they are. This is precisely the reason why you have low confidence. When you're not thankful for being who you are, and for the skills and talents you have, you are giving yourself permission to be unhappy. When you are unhappy, low confidence kicks in.

Low confidence, unhappiness, and lack of gratitude all go hand in hand. When you short circuit this whole thinking and emotional process by choosing to be thankful for everything you have and everything you are, you lay the foundation to gaining self-confidence.

2. Review your talents and strengths daily.

Everybody has talents and strengths. There is no person who is completely worthless. We are all blessed with some sort of talent or personal strength. You are probably the best in the world at something, no matter how obscure. Your great project is to honestly assess your list of talents and strengths and review them every day. Be thankful that you have them. Always remind yourself that you have these to offer the world. Even write them on a little card and put them into your wallet so you can remind yourself of what you can offer in the hardest of times.

3. Visualize the worst-case scenario... and realize that they're not so horrible.

Regardless of the area in your life that you have low confidence about, think of the worst-case situation.

What are the real downsides and negative consequences? Give yourself permission to realize that if worse comes to worst, things aren't that bad. For example, if you are afraid of trying to sell people on something, think about the worst thing that can happen.

What's the worst that can happen? You go home with no money in your hand. You probably are doing that already, so things aren't really that bad, right? The worst-case scenario may have already happened, and here you are still alive and reading this book.

Let this give you confidence that failure will only help you, and won't tear you down at all. Look at the worst-case scenario, and free yourself from the fear of it.

4. What are you missing out on due to your lack of confidence?

When you compare the kind of life you could be living if you had more confidence your present situation... how does that make you feel?

You would undoubtedly realize that you have a lot more to gain. You would realize that you really don't have that much to lose if you put in the kind of time, effort, and discipline to gain the confidence you lack. Above all else, you might realize that your hunger for your desired life is far greater than your insecurities holding you back.

You should perform this cost-benefit analysis on a daily basis. Eventually, you will get off the fence and put in the right kind of effort, focus, and energy you need to gain the confidence that you need to live the life that you are capable of living.

As an extreme example, what if you had a huge fear of talking to strangers yet needed to ask for directions or else you would starve? Sometimes overcoming your lack of confidence is not just beneficial, but necessary.

5. Adopt positivity.

It's easy to say you should adopt positivity.

The reality is that you already know how to be positive. The simple fact you're alive and haven't killed yourself is an act of positivity.

Your job is to simply water that seed of positivity so that it grows into a massive tree of positive thoughts, mental energy and attitude. We are all positive already just by the mere fact that we hung on another day. Hang on to this realization, and milk it for all the positivity that you can get. Of course, this ties closely to gratitude and being thankful for what you have on a daily basis.

6. Avoid comparing yourself to others.

The surest way to become miserable is to compare yourself to others. I don't care about how much money you have, how good-looking you are, or how awesome your car is. The moment you compare yourself to others, you are setting in motion negative forces that would lead to you feeling crappy about yourself. There are always bound to be people better than you in any regard.

So what? Does that make them happier? No.

Comparison to others can only lead to personal unhappiness. Instead, compare yourself to what you could be if you had a higher level of confidence.

7. Fake it 'til you make it.

I'm not a fan of this over-used piece of advice, but it does seem to resonate with some people. A simple method to gain self-confidence is to act confident. Start talking confidently, start thinking confidently. In other words, start acting like a confident person.

When you start the process of projecting the reality that you would like to live, other people will start responding to you as a truly confident person, and then you would start to internalize this reality. Eventually, you would stop faking it because it has become real. Somebody has to make that first step. The worst thing that you can do is to wait until somebody makes that decision for you. You have to do it yourself.

8. Eliminate negative influences and people.

It's hard to soar like an eagle when you surround yourself with turkeys. If you are surrounding yourself with people who are negative and who hate themselves, chances are you will continue to feel crappy about yourself and never achieve the level of confidence you need to achieve.

Instead, hang out with people who you know are confident. Soak up their energy levels, soak up their signals and bounce it back to them. This way, they inspire you to become a better person instead of enabling you to accept mediocrity, defeat, and frustration.

You are the sum of the five people you spend the most time with, so choose them carefully. Let them lift you up with their own successes and ambitions.

9. Avoid perfectionism.

While I did advise you to compare yourself to your ideal, make sure that the ideal is not perfect. Make sure that you do this in a way that avoids perfectionism. It's one thing to have an ideal to strive for, it's another to feel dejected when you don't meet that ideal.

Perfectionism is simply the act of beating yourself up because you don't measure up to something that doesn't exist.

Understand the proper uses of ideals and benchmarks, and avoid perfectionism.

10. Let go of what you can't control.

There are many aspects of your life that you simply cannot control. Be at peace with that. Focus instead on the things you can control, and don't let other things damage your confidence. How can it be a reflection of you and your confidence if you can't control it?

You can control how you act, you can control how you respond to things. You can't control what other people think about you and you can't control the past. Let go of those things and focus on what you can control to increase your confidence.

11. Take pride in your appearance.

If you want to feel good about yourself, you must like what you see in the mirror. If you feel like a bum, stop looking like a bum.

Don't be afraid to put a little effort in – who is going to make fun of you for wanting to improve yourself? Get a haircut, buy better clothes, and practice better hygiene. When that person looking back at the mirror looks better, you feel better about yourself, and then that person can start looking even better.

Sound shallow? Too bad, that's the world we live in. Hate the game, not the player.

By following all these steps, you can boost your self-confidence to a high enough level that it maintains itself on auto pilot. What's important is to take that first decisive step today. Nobody's going to give you confidence – it's something that you choose and maintain by yourself.

17. Six confidence-destroying mindsets to rid yourself of.

I don't need to tell you this, but a lack of confidence is almost completely mental.

There are actually **specific thought patterns** that can lead to low confidence on a daily basis, and I hope to identify these for you so that you can recognize and overcome them. It's tough to recognize how damaging our own thoughts might be to ourselves without some outside perspective.

After all, if we're always stuck in a particular mode of thought, how are we to know that there is different or better? Sometimes it just takes shining a light on your negative habits and inaccurate perceptions to completely change them and smash through your fears and goals.

1. All or nothing conclusions.

This is when every result is black and white, right of wrong, light and dark. You split every situation or scenario into a false dilemma, where there is only one correct answer – if you don't get it, you are wrong, and your confidence plummets. This incorrectly perceives the world as without shades of gray, where a conclusion may not even be tied to you at all. Sometimes, the answer is maybe and it's not your fault.

2. Overgeneralization.

This is when you take an experience and generalize the outcome so that anything similar will have the same outcome. You make a broad conclusion based on one factor, and predict that it either says something about you, or that you have no ability to change things.

For example, if you spend a lot of time at home, perhaps you feel that this is because you have few friends... and thus you spend a lot of time at home alone.

Overgeneralization can be particularly hurtful to your confidence because it can glue you into a thought pattern where you are never good enough... all on the basis of one instance or outcome.

3. Magnification.

This is when you give proportionally greater weight to a failure or perceived failure, so that it makes it seem like all of your experiences end with failure. This is obviously untrue, and serves to cloud your judgment and make it difficult to objectively view your strengths and accomplishments – which as I've discussed, is important to establishing a baseline confidence internally.

4. Minimization.

On the flip side, this is when you give proportionally lesser weight to a success of perceived success or strength of yours. It can be seen as an overabundance of modesty, but you might actually believe that you have accomplished nothing. You may even believe that any success was not due to you, just a stroke of luck or other people's help.

This has the same effect of magnification, where you cannot truly see what strengths you actually possess, which makes you feel like you have nothing to tie your confidence to. This is a difficult step to overcome.

Notably, magnification and minimization can also occur in comparison to other people. Other people's positive characteristics will be magnified and their accomplishments tied to their skill, while your own positive traits will be minimized and your accomplishments tied to dumb luck.

5. Should statements.

This is when you feel that you should conform to a certain standard, either set by yourself or others, and often unrealistic. If you fail to do so, then you have fallen short and have failed.

Thinking in terms of "I should" or "they should" places duties on yourself or others that may not necessarily exist. Most of the time, they don't. So when you place expectations on yourself especially, you set yourself up for failure.

For example, if you believe that you "should" be able to solve a math problem in under 60 seconds, and you fail to do so – you have just directly undermined your math abilities and lowered your confidence in that area. Putting a strict requirement on yourself and then falling short can only be negative for your confidence, and is rarely ever a relevant standard.

6. Mislabeling.

This is a type of overgeneralization that I touched on before. This is when you mislabel the cause of your own successes and accomplishments. People will low confidence will more often than not label their accomplishments in terms of luck and other extrinsic factors, rather than intrinsic skill and attributes that would cause one to build confidence in that arena.

The mere use of mislabeling, when not used as false modesty, can indicate a deep commitment to low confidence. You simply can't see things in terms of your own abilities, and need to justify positive acts as a result of other things and people.

For example, if you were to increase your company's revenues by 20% one quarter, you would attribute that to market conditions, other people's efforts, dumb luck, and increased marketing efforts – nothing directly from you. Don't be afraid to seize your moments.

Conclusion

Here's hoping that you have gained a realistic and healthy perspective on what it means to be truly confident.

As I stated before, however, it's not just a matter of magically reading a book and embodying those special mindsets. It is very unlikely that a switch will simply flip, so confidence is also a process that requires some time and deliberate work.

Confidence is a concept that can transform lives, but must also come from within to be strong. I hope that you've taken my laws to heart and have begun working on bringing your confidence from within.

Sincerely,

Patrick King
Dating and Social Skills Coach
www.PatrickKingConsulting.com

P.S. If you enjoyed this book, please don't be shy and

drop me a line, leave a review, or both! I love reading feedback, and reviews are the lifeblood of Kindle books, so they are always welcome and greatly appreciated.

Other books by Patrick King include:

CHATTER: Small Talk, Charisma, and How to Talk to Anyone http://www.amazon.com/dp/B00J5HH2Y6

Magnetic: How to Impress, Connect, and Influence
http://www.amazon.com/dp/B00ON8WJKY

Social Fluency: Genuine Social Habits to Work a Room, Own a Conversation, and be Instantly Likeable... Even Introverts!
http://www.amazon.com/dp/B00PJBF6JK

Cheat Sheet

Law 1. Confidence is the gateway emotion.

Confidence is the one emotion and mindset that allows all of your other positive traits to shine through. Without it, you may as well have no redeeming features, simply because people won't be able to see them.

Law 2. Confidence creates magnetism.

People are attracted to others with confidence be it out of latent jealousy, inspiration, or just a pleasurable interaction. Be that person.

Law 3. Diagnose your confidence drainers.

Introspect exactly what you feel insecure about and learn to leave them in the past. Don't confuse a judgment on your abilities with unfortunate circumstances.

Law 4. Recognize and defeat imposter syndrome.

Imposter syndrome is when you don't feel that you deserve your accolades, that everyone around you is far smarter, and that you are only where you are by a stroke of luck. Learn to love yourself and tie your accomplishments to your actual abilities.

Law 5. Draw confidence internally.

Confidence that depends on external validation puts you at the mercy of other people and is dangerously unstable. Only you can make yourself your first priority.

Law 6. Catalog your strengths and ACTUAL weaknesses.

Far too often, we misperceive that we are terrible at everything and good at nothing. Objectively introspect and catalog what you are good at and can be confident about – and what your ACTUAL weaknesses are.

Law 7. Perfection is an utter myth.

Holding yourself to an impossible standard is unhealthy and causes insecurity where it shouldn't exist. No one is perfect, and no one expects it of you – so why do you expect it of yourself?

Law 8. Vulnerability displays supreme confidence.

If you can own your flaws and vulnerabilities and become secure in them, then you can start owning your strengths and building your confidence. Vulnerability requires a supreme level of confidence and comfort with oneself.

Law 9. Choose to be confident on a daily basis.

Make a conscious choice to try to embody confidence and positivity and observe the feedback and signals you receive from others help grow your confidence.

Law 10. Preparation guarantees confidence.

If you prepare for certain situations where insecurity lurks, you can guarantee a certain amount of confidence and level of success. Do this often and watch the confidence transfer over to other areas of your life.

Law 11. Run towards failure.

Failure is one of the best teachers, and the best lesson it can teach you is that failure doesn't end the world. You can overcome it, and not fearing failure is a keystone of confidence.

Law 12. Practice confidence to gain it.

Take a proactive stance towards confidence and focus on small daily mindsets that will help you embody an overall confident approach to life.

Law 13. Incremental goals stack confidence.

Begin with small accomplishments, and gradually grow the challenges involved so that you have a certain level of mastery over situations. Watch your confidence grow and spill over to other situations.

Law 14. Look good to feel good.

It's a shallow world. If you look good, you will feel more confident and empowered in your own skin. You will also be treated differently by the world, which will increase your confidence.

Law 15. Physical acts create physiological confidence.

Studies have shown that simply committing to emulating a confident person's actions can cause physiological and mental changes that make confidence literally a part of you.

Made in the USA
San Bernardino, CA
18 August 2016